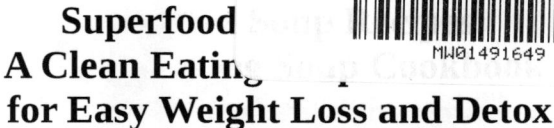

Superfood
A Clean Eating for Easy Weight Loss and Detox

by **Vesela Tabakova**

Text copyright(c)2017 Vesela Tabakova

All rights reserved. No part of this publication may be reproduced, distributed, or transmitted in any form or by any means, including photocopying, recording, or other electronic or mechanical methods, without the prior written permission of the publisher, except in the case of brief quotations embodied in critical reviews and certain other noncommercial uses permitted by copyright law.

Although every precaution has been taken to verify the accuracy of the information contained herein, the author and publisher assume no responsibility for any errors or omissions. No liability is assumed for damages that may result from the use of information contained within.

Table Of Contents

Superfoods in Our Backyard	5
My Favorite Superfood Ingredients:	7
Superfood Herbs and Spices in My Recipes	12
Chicken Soup with Buckwheat	14
Lemon Chicken and Kale Soup	15
Slow Cooker French-style Farmhouse Chicken Soup	16
Chicken Vegetable Soup	17
Slow Cooker Chicken Noodle Soup	18
Chicken and Ricotta Meatball Soup	19
Asian-style Chicken Soup	20
Bean and Chicken Soup	21
Lemon Chicken Soup with Quinoa	22
Chicken Quinoa Soup	23
Slow Cooker Chicken Broccoli Soup	24
Slow Cooker Sausage, Spinach and Tomato Soup	25
Lentil, Ground Beef and Quinoa Soup	26
Hearty Lamb and Root Vegetables Soup	27
Meatball and Chickpea Soup	28
Beef Noodle Soup	30
Cabbage, Beef and Buckwheat Soup	31
Italian Wedding Soup	32
Italian Meatball Soup	34
Easy Fish Soup	36
Dump Bean and Bacon Soup	38
Fish and Noodle Soup	39
Roasted Brussels Sprout and Cauliflower Soup	40
Roasted Brussels Sprout and Sweet Potato Soup	41
Broccoli, Zucchini and Blue Cheese Soup	43
Beetroot and Carrot Soup	44
Baked Beet and Apple Soup	45
Vegetarian Borscht	46
Spiced Parsnip Soup	47
Pumpkin and Chickpea Soup	48
Brussels Sprout and Potato Soup	49
Brussels Sprout and Tomato Soup	50

Potato, Carrot and Zucchini Soup	51
Leek, Rice and Potato Soup	52
Lightly Spiced Carrot and Chickpea Soup	53
Carrot and Ginger Soup	54
Sweet Potato Soup	55
Irish Carrot Soup	56
Lentil, Buckwheat and Mushroom Soup	57
Cream of Wild Mushroom Soup	58
Mediterranean Chickpea and Tomato Soup	59
French-style Vegetable Soup	60
Minted Pea and Potato Soup	61
Brussels Sprout and Lentil Soup	62
Moroccan Lentil Soup	63
Curried Lentil Soup	64
Green Lentil Soup with Rice	65
Simple Black Bean Soup	66
Bean and Pasta Soup	67
Slow Cooked Split Pea Soup	68
Spiced Citrus Bean Soup	69
Slow Cooker Tuscan-style Soup	70
Crock Pot Tomato Basil Soup	71
Chunky Minestrone	72
Cream of Tomato Soup	73
Cauliflower Soup	74
Creamy Artichoke Soup	75
Tomato Artichoke Soup	76
Creamy Artichoke and Horseradish Soup	77
Roasted Red Pepper Soup	78
Vietnamese Noodle Soup	79
Old-Fashioned Spinach Soup	80
Spinach, Nettle and Feta Cheese Soup	81
Nettle Soup	82
Celery Root Soup	83
Sweet Potato and Coconut Soup	84
Red Lentil and Quinoa Soup	85
Spinach, Leek and Quinoa Soup	86

Leek, Quinoa and Potato Soup	87
Garden Quinoa Soup	88
Quinoa, White Bean, and Kale Soup	89
FREE BONUS RECIPES: 10 Natural Homemade Beauty Recipes that are Easy on the Budget	90
Dry Skin Body Scrub	91
Lavender Body Scrub Recipe	91
Rosemary Body Scrub	92
Banana-Sugar Body Scrub	92
Coffee Body Scrub	93
Strained Yogurt Face Mask	93
Oats Bran Face Mask	94
Pear and Honey Mask	94
Banana Nourishing Mask	95
Apple Autumn Mask	95
About the Author	96

Superfoods in Our Backyard

The foods we eat have an enormous impact on our body and mind. Some foods are really power foods because they not only provide energy to the body but heal and protect it from environmental hazards, aging and illness. The amazing thing I discovered recently is that we actually have plenty of power foods with surprising qualities around us – they are already in our kitchen or backyard. And while some foods get all the glory, recent research has shown that local, common foods we love and eat regularly have the same immunity-boosting, age-defying, fantastic super-powers. These superfoods are inexpensive, quick to cook, delicious, and easy to shop. In fact, most nuts and seeds, dark green vegetables, fatty fish, such as salmon, mackerel and sardines, vegetables with bright, dark or intense colors such as beets and their greens, eggplants, red peppers and tomatoes have potent superfood qualities. Legumes such as peanuts, lentils and beans; citrus fruit and berries, and whole grains are also among the most nutritious foods on the planet. |It is amazing that even the herbs that we grow in our backyards like oregano, basil or rosemary are so chock-full of phytonutrients, antioxidants and vitamins that they have the same healing powers as lots of over the counter medicines.

The reason these foods are frequently called superfoods is that they nourish your body on a very deep level and fight off a range of health disorders. The wonderful effects power foods have on your body can include lowering total cholesterol, regulating blood pressure and helping protect against heart disease or preventing inflammatory processes. Some superfoods are beneficial in fighting cancer cells, while others help protect organs from toxins, promote digestive health, regulate metabolism and burn body fat. If you were to start eating a superfood rich diet today, you would soon see beneficial results. You will boost your immunity, your skin and hair will glow, your nails will grow, your will drop a few pounds and, more importantly, you will feel younger and more energetic.

The soup recipes I have collected for you are all prepared with superfood ingredients and are rich in nutrients that you should be eating every day. They are inexpensive, delicious and easy to prepare.

My Favorite Superfood Ingredients:

Alliums

Leeks, onions, garlic and chives have potent health-enhancing qualities. Research shows that they can help lower blood pressure and cholesterol levels, inhibit the growth of prostate, stomach, and colon cancer cells, and have antibiotic and immune-boosting properties.

Asparagus

Asparagus is very low calorie (only 21 calories in a serving) but is a very good source of folate, vitamin K, vitamins A and C. It is also high in lycopene, a phytonutrient that helps protect cells and other structures in the body from oxygen damage and has cancer-preventing properties. In addition, asparagus is a prebiotic food because it contains inulin, a fiber nourishing to good gut bacteria that line our intestinal tract.

Avocados

Avocados contain the best kind of fats and are extremely good in blocking the absorption of bad fats. Adding them to your diet will aid the body's blood and tissue regeneration, will stabilize blood sugar levels and help prevent heart disorders. In addition to good fats avocados are high in fiber, folate. potassium, vitamin E, and magnesium. They're also high in lutein, which aids eyesight.

Beans

Beans are pretty much the perfect food - high in protein and loaded with fiber, low in cholesterol, and high in folate, iron and magnesium. Eating beans can help lower cholesterol levels and reduce the risk of certain cancers. And because beans are naturally low fat and low calorie, adding them to your diet can cut down the calories without making you feel deprived. Even one of the more calorific bean varieties, contains only 33 calories per ounce.

Beets

The pigment betacyanin, which gives beets their distinctive hue, is just one of several disease-fighting phytonutrients found in this root vegetable. Beets are also a good source of folate, which guards against birth defects, colon cancer, and osteoporosis. They are also high in fiber and beta-carotene.

Broccoli, cabbage, cauliflower

Cruciferous vegetables - cabbages, cauliflower, broccoli contain a powerful range of disease fighting nutrients. They all contain chemicals which have been shown to reduce the risk of lung, colon, breast, ovarian, and bladder cancer. Cruciferous vegetables provide significant cardiovascular benefits as well.

Red cabbage stimulates the immune system, kills bacteria and viruses, and is a good blood purifier. It is rich in anthocyanins which are the same pigment molecules that make blueberries blue and are another powerful antioxidant.

Eating broccoli is great for your hair, skin, and teeth as the vegetable contains more vitamin C than an orange and as much calcium as a glass of milk. It is also a good source of folate which is necessary for the production and maintenance of new cells. Broccoli is also a great source of fiber, potassium, iron and vitamin K. Vitamin K is known to be important for blood coagulation and for maintaining proper bone density. It also plays a key role in the proper development of the fetus.

Buckwheat

While many people think that buckwheat is a cereal grain, it is actually a seed like quinoa. That's why it is a suitable substitute for grains for people with celiac disease, gluten allergies, or anyone trying to avoid gluten. Buckwheat tastes great - nutty and buttery, it is low on the glycemic index, has more protein than rice or wheat and is high in the amino acids lysine and arginine, both of which are essential for a healthy heart and strong immunity. Because it is also high in insoluble fiber, including buckwheat in your menu will help normalize cholesterol levels and reduce hypertension. And there is more: buckwheat has high triptofan levels and will help ensure a sound night's sleep. Magnesium and a natural flavonoid called rutin in buckwheat help to extend the activity of vitamin C and other antioxidant nutrients.

Dark, Leafy Greens

Dark, leafy greens such as spinach, kale, and Swiss chard are incredibly healthy. Low in calories and extremely high in nutrients, they have extraordinarily high levels of antioxidants and are therefore among the best cancer preventing foods. In addition, dark leafy greens are chock-full of vitamins A, C, E and K, Potassium , Magnesium, Iron, Calcium, Folate and many B-vitamins. Dark green leafy vegetables are also very high in fiber, therefore, adding them to your everyday menu is a great way to decrease calories without constantly feeling hungry.

Eggs

Eggs are the best protein source on the planet and outstrip milk, beef, whey, and soy in the quality of protein they provide. They are versatile, economical and nutritious. Egg yolks contain choline, which helps protect heart and brain function, memory, and prevents cholesterol and fat from accumulating in the liver.

Fish

Eating fish helps cut the risk of heart disease, stroke, cancer, Alzheimer's, diabetes, and arthritis. The fatty fish varieties may also help alleviate depression. Wild-caught salmon, herring, and sardines, are the ones that have the most superfood qualities.

Olive Oil

Olive oil is high in monosaturated fat, which has been found to lower blood cholesterol levels, decreasing the risk of heart disease. This type of oil keeps insulin levels low and improves the control of blood sugar. In addition, olive oil contains vitamin K, which aids blood clotting, and vitamin E, an antioxidant important in the creation of red blood cells. The Mediterranean diet, rich in olive oil, creates a lower incidence of heart disease, diabetes, colon cancer, asthma, and atherosclerosis.

Poultry

Poultry is the world's primary source of animal protein. Chicken and turkey offer a rich array of nutrients, particularly niacin, selenium, vitamins B6 and B12, and zinc. These nutrients are essential for a healthy heart and are also valuable in helping lower the risk for cancer.

Tomatoes

Some studies have indicated that incorporating tomatoes in your daily menu may help decrease the risk of prostate cancer, as well as breast, lung and stomach cancers. The reason tomatoes have these miracle qualities is the lycopene – a phytonutrient that has the ability to help protect cells and other structures in the body from oxygen damage and has been proven to have antioxidant and cancer-preventing properties. Lycopene is also good for preventing heart disease. Red tomatoes are the best, because they're packed with more lycopene; and processed tomatoes are just as potent as fresh ones, because it's easier for the body to absorb the lycopene.

Quinoa

Quinoa is the only exotic superfood in my list but I recently fell in love with it and I cannot stop experimenting with different ways to prepare and eat it. It is also one of the healthiest foods on the planet and I think that everyone should give it a try.

Quinoa is a small gluten free seed that is extremely high in protein, fiber, iron, zinc, vitamin E and selenium. It is the only plant-based protein that contains all nine essential amino acids we need for tissue development. These nine essential amino acids are the ones that your body cannot synthesize in quantities sufficient to sustain good health, so they need to come from food sources.

Recent studies have more great news for quinoa eaters. It seems that the processes of boiling, simmering, and steaming quinoa does not significantly compromise the quality of its fatty acids, allowing us to enjoy its cooked texture and flavor while maintaining its nutrient benefits. Food scientists have speculated that it is the diverse array of antioxidants found in quinoa that contribute to this oxidative protection.

Walnuts

Walnuts are rich in fiber, B vitamins, magnesium, selenium, and antioxidants such as Vitamin E. They are also contain more plant sterols and omega-3 fatty acids than any other nuts. Walnuts contain the most alpha-linolenic omega-3 fatty acids, which lower bad cholesterol and may reduce inflammation in arteries.

Yogurt

Like the milk it's made from, yogurt is loaded with calcium, iodine, riboflavin, and vitamin B2. Real yogurt also contains probiotics, the good bacteria your digestive system needs to process and benefit from all the other things you eat and fortify the immune system. Eating yogurt has the added benefit of lowering the bad cholesterol levels and preventing yeast infections.

Superfood Herbs and Spices in My Recipes

The herbs and spices I use in my recipes not only provide natural flavorings to make food more delicious, they are also an incredible source of antioxidants. The superstar herbs are:

Basil

It is a powerful antioxidant that prevents free radical damage, primary cause of heart disease, cancer, and many other serious health conditions, as well as aging. It is an excellent source of vitamin K, calcium, magnesium and beta carotene, manganese, vitamin C and potassium. Basil has amazing anti-inflammatory properties and extraordinary healing benefits that work for arthritis, allergies, and inflammatory bowel conditions.

Dried Red Peppers

Cayenne, crushed red peppers and paprika stimulate digestive enzymes, and help prevent stomach ulcers. Cayenne pepper also reduces bad cholesterol, triglyceride levels, and decreases the formation of harmful blood clots all of which prevent heart attacks and strokes. It is an effective anti-inflammatory and pain relief remedy for everything from headaches to sore muscles, as well as clearing nasal congestion and boosting immunity.

Oregano

It is among the highest in antioxidants of the dried herbs. Its high levels of antioxidants mean that a half teaspoon of dried oregano has the benefits of a spinach salad or three cups of chopped broccoli. Oregano has the added ability to act as an expectorant, clearing congestion, and can also improve digestion.

Rosemary

It contains potent antioxidants and anti-inflammatory agents. The carnosic acid found in rosemary has been shown to reduce stroke risk and shield brain cells from free-radical damage, which can worsen the effects of a stroke. In addition carnosic acid can protect against degenerative diseases like Alzheimer's and other general effects of aging. Adding rosemary to your diet can help improve concentration, boost memory, and lift depression. It can also strengthen the immune system, improve circulation and stimulate digestion.

Chicken Soup with Buckwheat

Serves 4

Ingredients:

1 lb boneless chicken thighs, cut in bite sized pieces

1/2 cup buckwheat

1 small onion, finely cut

2 carrots, grated

1 celery rib, finely cut

5 cups water

2 garlic cloves, chopped

1 bay leaf

1 tsp salt

1/2 tsp black pepper

1/2 cup fresh parsley, finely cut, to serve

4 tbsp lemon juice, to serve

Directions:

Heat a soup pot over medium heat. Gently sauté onion, garlic, carrot and celery, stirring occasionally.

Add in chicken, water and bay leaf and bring to a boil. Season with salt and black pepper and add in buckwheat.

Stir to combine and simmer for 30 minutes. Remove the bay leaf and serve with parsley and lemon juice.

Lemon Chicken and Kale Soup

Serves 5-6

Ingredients:

1 cup cooked chicken, cubed or shredded

1 small onion, chopped

1 small carrot, grated

1 bunch kale, cut into 1 inch pieces

4 cups chicken broth

1 tsp Worcestershire sauce

1 tsp Dijon mustard

3 tbsp olive oil

1 tsp paprika

3 tbsp lemon juice

1 tsp grated lemon zest

salt and black pepper, to taste

grated Parmesan cheese, to serve

Directions:

Heat a soup pot over medium heat. Gently sauté onion, garlic and carrot, stirring occasionally. Stir in the lemon zest, chicken broth, Worcestershire sauce, Dijon mustard and cooked chicken.

Bring to a boil then reduce heat and simmer for 10 minutes. Stir in the kale and simmer for 3-4 minutes or until kale is tender.

Stir in the lemon juice and season with salt and pepper to taste. Serve sprinkled with Parmesan cheese.

Slow Cooker French-style Farmhouse Chicken Soup

Serves 5-6

Ingredients:

4 skinless, boneless chicken thighs, cut into bite-sized pieces

1 leek, trimmed, halved, finely cut

1 celery rib, trimmed, halved, finely cut

2 carrots, chopped

1 fennel bulb, trimmed, diced

1 cup frozen peas

4 cups chicken broth

1 tsp thyme

1 tsp salt

Directions:

Combine all ingredients in the slow cooker. Cover and cook on low for 6-7 hours.

Chicken Vegetable Soup

Serves 6-7

Ingredients:

2 lb boneless chicken thighs, cut in bite sized pieces

1 small onion, chopped

1 celery rib, chopped

1/2 small parsnip, chopped

3 garlic cloves, chopped

1 carrot, chopped

1 red bell pepper, chopped

1 lb potatoes, peeled and cubed

5 cups chicken broth

1 tsp thyme

2 bay leaves

1 tsp salt

black pepper, to taste

1 tsp summer savory

Directions:

Season the chicken well with salt, ground black pepper and summer savory. Place it in a slow cooker with all remaining ingredients.

Cover and cook on low for 6-7 hours or on high for 4 hours.

Slow Cooker Chicken Noodle Soup

Serves 6-7

Ingredients:

2 lb boneless chicken thighs, cut in bite sized pieces

1 small onion, chopped

1 tomato, diced

1 red bell pepper, chopped

2-3 broccoli florets

4 cups chicken broth

2 cups wide egg noodles, uncooked

1 tsp garlic powder

1 tsp oregano

2 bay leaves

1 tsp salt

black pepper, to taste

Directions:

Season the chicken well with salt, black pepper garlic powder and oregano. Place it in a slow cooker with all remaining ingredients.

Cover and cook on low for 6-7 hours or on high for 4-5 hours.

Add noodles to slow cooker; cover and cook on low 20 minutes.

Chicken and Ricotta Meatball Soup

Serves 4-5

Ingredients:

1 lb ground chicken meat

1 egg, lightly whisked

1 cup whole milk ricotta

1 cup grated Parmesan cheese

2-3 tbsp flour

1/2 onion, chopped

4 cups chicken broth

2 cups baby spinach

1/2 tsp dried oregano

3 tbsp olive oil

½ tsp black pepper

Directions:

Place ground chicken, Ricotta, Parmesan, egg and black pepper in a bowl. Combine well with hands and roll teaspoonfuls of the mixture into balls.

Roll each meatball in the flour then set aside on a large plate.

In a deep soup pot, heat olive oil and gently sauté onion until transparent. Add in oregano and chicken broth and bring to a boil.

Add meatballs, reduce heat, and simmer, uncovered, for 15 minutes. Add in baby spinach leaves and simmer for 2 more minutes until it wilts.

Asian-style Chicken Soup

Serves 4-5

Ingredients:

1 roasted chicken, skin and bones removed, shredded

1/2 Chinese cabbage, shredded

5 cups chicken broth

1 cup water

1 red chili, thinly sliced

2 carrots, peeled and cut into short, thin sticks

4 oz fresh shiitake mushrooms, sliced

16 oz snow peas, shredded lengthwise

2 tbsp soy sauce

1/4 cup coriander leaves, finely cut

Directions:

Combine the chicken broth, water, soy sauce and the chili in a deep soup pot. Gently bring to a boil then add in carrots, mushrooms, snow peas and shredded chicken.

Reduce heat and simmer for 3-4 minutes. Add the cabbage and cook for 2 minutes or until the cabbage wilts. Stir the coriander into soup. Divide soup between bowls and serve.

Bean and Chicken Soup

Serves 6-7

Ingredients:

3 bacon strips, diced

2 cups chicken, cooked and cut in small pieces

1 cup kidney beans, rinsed and drained

1 big onion, chopped

2 garlic cloves, crushed

4 cups water

1 cup canned tomatoes, diced, undrained

1 bay leaf

1 tsp dried thyme

1 tsp savory

½ tsp dried basil

salt and pepper, to taste

Directions:

Cook the onion and bacon over medium heat for 2-3 minutes. Add the garlic and cook for a minute more. Add in water, tomatoes and seasonings and bring to a boil.

Cover, reduce heat and simmer for 30 minutes. Add the chicken and beans. Simmer for 5 minutes. Serve warm.

Lemon Chicken Soup with Quinoa

Serves 4-5

Ingredients:

1.2 oz uncooked boneless, skinless chicken breast, diced

1/3 cup quinoa

3 cups chicken broth

1 cup water

1 onion, finely diced

2 raw eggs

3 tbsp olive oil

1/2 cup fresh lemon juice

1 tsp salt

1/2 tsp ground black pepper

1/2 cup finely cut parsley, to serve

Directions:

In a medium pot, heat the olive oil and sauté the onions until they are soft and translucent. Add in chicken broth, water, diced chicken and washed quinoa.

Bring to a boil, reduce heat and simmer for 20 minutes or until the chicken is cooked through.

In a small bowl, beat the eggs and lemon juice together. Pour two cups of broth slowly into the egg mixture, whisking constantly. When all the broth is incorporated, add this mixture back into the pot of chicken soup and stir well to blend. Do not boil any more.

Season with salt and pepper and garnish with parsley. Serve hot.

Chicken Quinoa Soup

Serves 4

Ingredients:

2 chicken breasts

1/2 cup quinoa, rinsed

1 onion, chopped

2 cloves garlic, chopped

1 celery rib, chopped

1-2 carrots, cut

1 tsp paprika

1 bay leaf

10 black olives, pitted and halved

3 cups chicken broth

2 cups water

1/2 tsp dried oregano

salt and pepper, to taste

lemon juice, to serve

Directions:

Heat olive oil in a large soup pot and gently sauté onions, carrots, celery, garlic and oregano. Add in broth, water, the chicken breasts and olives and bring to the boil. Reduce heat and simmer slowly until cooked through.

Remove chicken, cut it in cubes and set aside in a bowl. Add quinoa to the soup and simmer for 10 minutes, then return the chicken and serve.

Slow Cooker Chicken Broccoli Soup

Serves 6-7

Ingredients:

2 lb boneless chicken thighs, cut in bite sized pieces

1 small onion, chopped

1 fresh garlic clove

6-7 fresh or frozen broccoli florets

4 cups chicken broth

2 potatoes, peeled and cubed

3 tbsp olive oil

1 tsp garlic powder

1 tsp dried oregano

1 tsp salt

black pepper, to taste

12 oz cheddar cheese, to serve

Directions:

In a skillet, saute onion and garlic with olive oil until onion is translucent.

Season the chicken well with salt, black pepper, garlic powder and oregano. Place it in slow cooker with the onion mixture and all remaining ingredients.

Cover and cook on low for 8-10 hours or on high for 4-5 hours. Serve topped with cheddar cheese.

Slow Cooker Sausage, Spinach and Tomato Soup

Serves 4-5

Ingredients:

1 lb ground sweet Italian sausage

1 lb spinach, frozen

4 large carrots, chopped

1 can red beans

1 jar pasta sauce

1 small onion, finely cut

1-2 cloves garlic, crushed

1 carrot, chopped

3 cups vegetable broth

1 tbsp paprika

1 tsp dried mint

salt and black pepper, to taste

Directions:

Brown the sausage in a pan.

Add the sausage and all the other ingredients to the slow cooker and cook on low for 6-8 hours.

Lentil, Ground Beef and Quinoa Soup

Serves 4-5

Ingredients:

1 lb ground beef

1/2 cup quinoa

1/1 cup green lentils

1 carrot, chopped

1 onion, chopped

1 small potato, peeled and diced

2-3 garlic cloves, chopped

2 tomatoes, grated or pureed

5 cups water

1 tsp summer savory or dried mint

1 tsp paprika

2 tbsp olive oil

1 tsp salt

ground black pepper, to taste

Directions:

Heat olive oil in a large soup pot. Brown the ground beef, breaking it up with a spoon. Add in paprika and garlic and stir. Add lentils, washed quinoa, remaining vegetables, water and spice.

Bring the soup to a boil. Reduce heat to low and simmer, covered, for about 40 minutes, or until the lentils are tender. Stir occasionally.

Hearty Lamb and Root Vegetables Soup

Serves 6-7

Ingredients:

2 cups roasted lamb, shredded

3 cups chicken or vegetable broth

1 cup water

1 cup canned tomatoes, diced, undrained

1 onion, chopped

1 large carrot, chopped

1 medium parsnip, peeled and chopped

1 small turnip, chopped

1 celery rib

3 tbsp olive oil

salt and black pepper, to taste

Directions:

Gently heat olive oil in a large saucepan and sauté onion, carrot, parsnip, celery and turnip, stirring, for 5 minutes, or until softened.

Add in lamb, broth, tomatoes, and a cup of water. Bring to the boil then reduce heat and simmer for 20 minutes, or until vegetables are tender. Season with salt and black pepper to taste.

Meatball and Chickpea Soup

Serves 4-5

Ingredients:

1 lb lean ground beef

3-4 tbsp flour

1 small onion, chopped

1 garlic clove, chopped

1 can tomatoes, diced and undrained

1 can chickpeas, drained

1 green pepper, chopped

4 cups water

½ bunch of parsley, finely cut

3 tbsp olive oil

½ tsp black pepper

1 tsp dried mint

1 tsp paprika

1 tsp salt

Directions:

Combine ground meat, paprika, black pepper and salt in a large bowl. Mix well with hands and roll teaspoonfuls of the mixture into balls. Put flour in a small bowl and roll each meatball in the flour, coating entire surface then set aside on a large plate.

Heat olive oil into a large soup pot and gently sauté onion, garlic and pepper until tender. Add water and tomatoes and bring to the boil over high heat. Add in meatballs and chickpeas.

Reduce heat to low and simmer, uncovered, for 25 minutes. Add mint and stir. Serve with lemon juice.

Beef Noodle Soup

Serves 7-8

Ingredients:

8 oz fillet steak, thinly sliced

6 oz rice stick noodles

2 carrots, peeled, halved, sliced diagonally

1 red pepper, deseeded, thinly sliced diagonally

7-8 spring onions, chopped

8 oz green beans, sliced diagonally

3 tbsp sweet chilli sauce

4 cups beef broth

1 tbsp olive oil

Directions:

In a skillet, heat olive oil and cook beef, stirring, until medium rare.

Place broth and half the onions in a saucepan over high heat. Bring to the boil, cover, reduce heat to low. Simmer for 5 minutes then add carrots, pepper and beans. Bring to the boil, uncovered. Cook for 2 minutes or until vegetables are tender. Remove from heat.

Stir in remaining onions and sweet chili sauce.

Place noodles in a heatproof bowl. Cover with boiling water. Stand for 5 minutes or until tender. Drain. Divide noodles between bowls. Top with beef. Ladle over boiling soup mixture. Serve.

Cabbage, Beef and Buckwheat Soup

Serves 7-8

Ingredients:

3/4 – 1 lb beef, chuck (boneless, cut into 1 inch cubes)

1 cup buckwheat

2 cups chopped cabbage

1 small onion, chopped

2 carrots, peeled, halved, sliced diagonally

1 red pepper, deseeded, thinly sliced diagonally

1 tbsp paprika

4 cups beef broth

1 tbsp olive oil

1/2 cup sour cream, to serve, optional

salt and black pepper, to taste

Directions:

In a deep soup pot, heat olive oil and cook beef, stirring, until lightly browned.

Add broth, paprika, onion and carrot and bring to the boil. Cover, reduce heat to low and simmer for 20 minutes then add the pepper, cabbage and buckwheat.

Bring to the boil and cook for 15 minutes or until vegetables are tender. Remove from heat.

Season with salt and pepper to taste and serve with sour cream.

Italian Wedding Soup

Serves 4-5

Ingredients:

1 lb lean ground beef

1/3 cup breadcrumbs

1 egg, lightly beaten

1 onion, grated

2 carrots, chopped

1 small head escarole, trimmed and cut into 1/2 inch strips

1 cup baby spinach leaves

1 cup small pasta

2 tbsp Parmesan cheese, grated

2 tbsp parsley, finely cut

1 tsp salt

1 tsp ground black pepper

3 tbsp olive oil

3 cups chicken broth

3 cups water

1 tsp dried oregano

Directions:

Combine ground beef, egg, onion, breadcrumbs, cheese, parsley, 1/2 teaspoon of the salt and 1/2 teaspoon of the black pepper. Mix well with hands. Using a tablespoon, make walnut sized meatballs. Heat olive oil in a large skillet and brown meatballs in batches. Place aside on a plate.

In a large soup pot boil broth and water together with carrots, oregano, and the remaining salt and pepper. Gently add meatballs. Reduce heat and simmer for 30 minutes. Add pasta, spinach and escarole and simmer 10 minutes more.

Italian Meatball Soup

Serves 6-7

Ingredients:

1 lb lean ground beef

1 small onion, grated

1 onion, chopped

2 garlic cloves, crushed

½ cup breadcrumbs

3-4 basil leaves, finely chopped

1/3 cup Parmesan cheese, grated

1 egg, lightly beaten

2 cups tomato sauce with basil

3 cups water

½ cup small pasta

1 zucchini, diced

½ cup green beans, trimmed, cut into thirds

2 tbsp olive oil

Directions:

Combine ground meat, grated onion, garlic, breadcrumbs, basil, Parmesan and egg in a large bowl. Season with salt and pepper. Mix well with hands and roll tablespoonfuls of the mixture into balls. Place on a large plate.

Heat olive oil into a large deep saucepan and sauté onion and garlic until transparent. Add tomato sauce, water, and bring to the boil over high heat. Add meatballs.

Reduce heat to medium-low and simmer, uncovered, for 10 minutes. Add in pasta and cook for 5 more minutes. Add the zucchini and beans. Cook until pasta and vegetables are tender. Serve sprinkled with Parmesan.

Easy Fish Soup

Serves 6-7

Ingredients:

1 lb white fish fillets cut in small pieces

9 oz scallops

1 onion, chopped

4 tomatoes, chopped

3 potatoes, diced

1 red pepper, chopped

2 carrots, diced

1 garlic clove, crushed

a bunch of fresh parsley

3 tbsp olive oil

a pinch of cayenne pepper

1 tsp dried oregano

1 tsp dried thyme

1 tsp dried dill

½ tsp pepper

½ cup white wine

4 cups water

1/3 cup heavy cream

Directions:

Heat the olive oil over medium heat and sauté the onion, red pepper, garlic and carrots until tender. Stir in the cayenne, herbs, salt, and pepper. Add the white wine, water, potatoes and tomatoes and bring to a boil.

Reduce heat, cover, and cook until the potatoes are almost done. Stir in the fish and the scallops and cook for another 10 minutes. Stir in the heavy cream and parsley and serve hot.

Dump Bean and Bacon Soup

Serves 5-6

Ingredients:

1 slices bacon, chopped

1 can Black Beans, rinsed

1 can Kidney Beans, rinsed

1 celery rib, chopped

1/2 red onion, chopped

1 can tomatoes, diced, undrained

4 cups water

1 tsp smoked paprika

1 tsp dried mint

1/2 cup fresh parsley

ground black pepper, to taste

Directions:

Dump all ingredients in a soup pot. Stir well and bring to a boil. Reduce heat and simmer for 35 minutes.

Season with salt and black pepper to taste, and serve.

Fish and Noodle Soup

Serves 4-5

Ingredients:

14 oz firm white fish, cut into strips

2 carrots, cut into ribbons

1 zucchini, cut into thin ribbons

7 oz white button mushrooms, sliced

1 celery rib, finely cut

1 cup baby spinach

7 oz fresh noodles

3 cups chicken broth

2 cups water

2 tbsp soy sauce

1/2 tsp ground ginger

black pepper, to taste

Directions:

Place chicken broth, water and soy sauce in a large saucepan. Bring to a boil and add in carrots, celery, zucchini, mushrooms, ginger and noodles.

Cook, partially covered, for 3-4 minutes then add in fish and simmer for 3 minutes or until the fish is cooked through. Add baby spinach and simmer, stirring, for 1 minute, or until it wilts. Season with black pepper and serve.

Roasted Brussels Sprout and Cauliflower Soup

Serves 4

Ingredients:

1 onion, finely chopped

2 garlic cloves, crushed

16 oz cauliflower florets

16 oz Brussels sprouts, halved

4 cups vegetable broth

6 tbsp olive oil

salt and pepper, to taste

Parmesan cheese, to serve

Directions:

Preheat oven to 450F.

Line a large baking sheet and place the cauliflower and Brussels sprouts on it. Drizzle with half the olive oil and roast on the bottom third of the oven for 30 minutes, or until slightly browned.

Heat the remaining oil in a saucepan over medium heat and sauté the onion and garlic, stirring, for 2-3 minutes or until soft.

Add in vegetable broth and bring to the boil then simmer 3-4 minutes. Stir in roasted vegetables and cook for 5 minutes more.

Set aside to cool then blend in batches and reheat. Serve sprinkled with Parmesan cheese.

Roasted Brussels Sprout and Sweet Potato Soup

Serves 4

Ingredients:

4 Italian Sausages

1 onion, finely chopped

2 garlic cloves, crushed

2 carrots, chopped

1 large sweet potato, peeled and chopped

16 oz Brussels sprouts, shredded

4 cups vegetable broth

4 tbsp olive oil

1 tsp paprika

1 tsp dried oregano

salt and pepper, to taste

Directions:

Preheat oven to 450F.

Line a large baking sheet and place the Brussels sprouts on it. Drizzle with half the olive oil and season with salt and pepper to taste. Roast on the bottom third of the oven for 20 minutes, or until golden.

Remove the sausage from the casing and brown it in a saucepan. Set aside in a plate.

In the same saucepan, heat the remaining oil over medium heat and sauté the onion, carrots, and garlic, stirring, for 2-3 minutes or until soft. Add paprika and stir to combine.

Add in the vegetable broth, sweet potato, oregano and sausage meat. Bring to the boil then simmer 15 minutes or until vegetables are tender.

Stir in roasted Brussels sprouts and cook for 5 minutes more.

Broccoli, Zucchini and Blue Cheese Soup

Serves 4-5

Ingredients:

2 leeks, white part only, sliced

1 head broccoli, coarsely chopped

2 zucchinis, peeled and chopped

1 potato, peeled and chopped

2 cups vegetable broth

3 cups water

3 tbsp olive oil

3.5 oz blue cheese, crumbled

1/3 cup light cream

salt and pepper, to taste

Directions:

Heat the oil in a large saucepan over medium heat. Sauté the leeks, stirring, for 5 minutes or until soft.

Add in bite sized pieces of broccoli, zucchinis and potato. Stir in the water and broth and bring to a boil.

Reduce heat to low and simmer, stirring occasionally, for 15 minutes, or until vegetables are just tender. Remove from heat and set aside for 5 minutes to cool slightly.

Transfer soup to a blender. Add in the cheese and blend in batches until smooth. Return to saucepan and place over low heat. Add cream and stir to combine. Season with salt and pepper to taste.

Beetroot and Carrot Soup

Serves 6

Ingredients:

4 beets, washed and peeled

2 carrots, peeled, chopped

2 potatoes, peeled, chopped

1 medium onion, chopped

2 cups vegetable broth

3 cups water

2 tbsp yogurt

2 tbsp olive oil

salt and pepper, to taste

a bunch or spring onions, finely cut, to serve

Directions:

Peel and chop the beets. Heat the olive oil in a saucepan over medium high heat and sauté the onion and carrot until tender.

Add in beets, potatoes, broth and water. Bring to the boil.

Reduce heat to medium and simmer, partially covered, for 30-40 minutes, or until the beets are tender.

Set aside to cool slightly.

Blend the soup in batches until smooth. Return it to pan over low heat and cook, stirring, for 4-5 minutes or until heated through. Season with salt and pepper to taste. Serve topped with yogurt and sprinkled with spring onions.

Baked Beet and Apple Soup

1.5 lb fresh beets, peeled and grated

2 carrots, chopped

1 onion, chopped

2 apples, peeled and chopped

1 tbsp sugar

1 bay leaf

2 tbs lemon juice

3 cups vegetable broth

3 tbsp olive oil

1 cup heavy cream

a bunch of fresh parsley, chopped, to serve

salt and black pepper, to taste

Directions:

Preheat the oven to 350 F. Toss the beets, apples, onion and carrots in olive oil and arrange in a casserole dish.

Add in the bay leaf and vegetable broth. Season with salt and pepper, cover with foil and bake for 1-2 hours. Discard the bay leaf and set aside to cool.

Blend everything in a blender, in batches, until smooth, then transfer to a large saucepan.

Season with salt and pepper to taste, stir in the cream and reheat without boiling. Serve the soup with a dollop of extra cream and sprinkled with chopped parsley.

Vegetarian Borscht

Serves 6

Ingredients:

4 beets, peeled, quartered

1 carrot, peeled, chopped

1 parsnip, peeled, cut into chunks

1 leek, white part only, sliced

1 onion, chopped

1/3 cup lemon juice

½ tsp nutmeg

3 bay leaves

6 cups vegetable broth

1 cup sour cream

2-3 dill springs, chopped

Directions:

Place the beets, carrot, parsnip, leek, onion, lemon juice, spices and bay leaves in a large saucepan with the vegetable broth.

Bring to the boil, then reduce the heat to low and simmer, partially covered, for 1 ½ hours.

Cool slightly, then blend in batches and season well with salt and pepper. Return to the saucepan and gently heat through. Place in bowls and garnish with sour cream and dill.

Spiced Parsnip Soup

Serves 4

Ingredients:

1.5 lb parsnips, peeled, chopped

2 onions, chopped

1 garlic clove

3 tbsp olive oil

1 tbs curry powder

½ cup heavy cream

salt and freshly ground pepper, to taste

Directions:

Sauté the onion and garlic together with the curry powder in a large saucepan. Stir in the parsnips and cook, stirring often, for 10 minutes.

Add in 5 cups of water, bring to the boil, and simmer for 30 minutes, or until the parsnips are tender.

Set aside to cool, then blend in batches until smooth. Return soup to pan over low heat and stir in the cream. Do not boil - only heat through. Season with salt and pepper.

Pumpkin and Chickpea Soup

Serves 6

Ingredients:

1 leek, white part only, thinly sliced

3 cloves garlic, finely chopped

2 carrots, peeled, coarsely chopped

2 lb pumpkin, peeled, deseeded, diced

1/3 cup chickpeas

½ tsp ground ginger

½ tsp ground cinnamon

½ tsp ground cumin

5 tbsp olive oil

Juice of ½ lemon

parsley springs, to serve

Directions:

Heat oil in a large saucepan and sauté leek, garlic and 2 tsp salt, stirring occasionally, until soft. Add cinnamon, ginger and cumin and stir. Add in carrots, pumpkin and chickpeas.

Add 5 cups of water to saucepan and bring to the boil, then reduce heat and simmer for 50 minutes or until the chickpeas are soft.

Remove from heat, add lemon juice and blend soup, in batches, until smooth. Return it to pan over low heat and cook, stirring, for 4-5 minutes, or until heated through. Serve topped with parsley sprigs.

Brussels Sprout and Potato Soup

Serves 4-5

Ingredients:

16 oz Brussels sprouts

2 potatoes, peeled and chopped

1 onion, chopped

3 garlic cloves, crushed

4 cups water

2 tbsp olive oil

creme fraiche, to serve

salt and black pepper, to taste

Directions:

Heat oil in a large saucepan over medium-high heat. Add onion and garlic and sauté, stirring, for 1-2 minutes until fragrant.

Add in Brussels sprouts, potatoes, rosemary and 4 cups of vegetable broth.

Cover and bring to the boil, then reduce heat to low. Simmer for 30 minutes, or until potatoes are tender.

Remove from heat. Blend until smooth. Return to pan. Cook for 4-5 minutes or until heated through. Season with salt and pepper and serve with creme fraiche.

Brussels Sprout and Tomato Soup

Serves 4-5

Ingredients:

16 oz Brussels sprouts

4 large tomatoes, diced

1 medium onion, chopped

3 garlic cloves, crushed

1 tsp sugar

2 cups vegetable broth

1 tbsp paprika

2 tbsp olive oil

salt and black pepper, to taste

Directions:

Heat oil in a deep soup pot over medium-high heat. Add onion, garlic and paprika and sauté, stirring, for 2-3 minutes or until soft.

Add in tomatoes and vegetable broth. Cover and bring to the boil, then reduce heat to low and simmer, stirring, for 10 minutes.

Remove from heat and blend until smooth. Return to pan. Stir in Brussels sprouts. Cook for 15 minutes more. Season with salt and pepper before serving.

Potato, Carrot and Zucchini Soup

Serves 4-5

Ingredients:

4-5 medium potatoes, peeled and diced

2 carrots, chopped

1 zucchini, peeled and chopped

1 celery rib, chopped

3 cups water

3 tbsp olive oil

1 cup whole milk

½ tsp dried rosemary

salt, to taste

black pepper, to taste

a bunch of fresh parsley for garnish, finely cut

Directions:

Heat the olive oil over medium heat and sauté the vegetables for 2-3 minutes. Add in 3 cups of water and the rosemary and bring the soup to a boil then lower heat and simmer until all the vegetables are tender.

Blend in a blender until smooth. Add a cup of warm milk and blend some more. Serve warm, seasoned with black pepper and sprinkled with parsley.

Leek, Rice and Potato Soup

Serves 4-5

Ingredients:

1/3 cup rice

4 cups of water

2-3 potatoes, peeled and diced

1 small onion, cut

1 leek halved lengthwise and sliced

3 tbsp olive oil

lemon juice, to serve

Directions:

Heat a soup pot over medium heat. Add olive oil and onion and sauté for 2 minutes. Add leeks and potatoes and cook for a few minutes more.

Add three cups of water, bring to a boil, reduce heat and simmer for 5 minutes. Add the very well washed rice and simmer for 10 minutes. Serve with lemon juice to taste.

Lightly Spiced Carrot and Chickpea Soup

Serves 4-5

Ingredients:

3-4 big carrots, chopped

1 leek, chopped

4 cups vegetable broth

1 cup canned chickpeas, undrained

½ cup orange juice

2 tbsp olive oil

½ tsp cumin

½ tsp ginger

4-5 tbsp yogurt, to serve

Directions:

Heat oil in a large saucepan over medium heat. Add in the leek and carrots and sauté until soft. Add orange juice, broth, chickpeas and spices.

Bring to the boil. Reduce heat to medium-low and simmer, covered, for 15 minutes. Blend soup until smooth, return to pan. Season with salt and pepper. Stir over heat until heated through. Pour in 4-5 bowls, top with yogurt and serve.

Carrot and Ginger Soup

Serves 4

Ingredients:

6 carrots, peeled and chopped

1 medium onion, chopped

4 cups water

3 tbsp olive oil

2 cloves garlic, minced

1 tbsp grated ginger

½ bunch fresh coriander, finely cut

salt and black pepper, to taste

½ cup heavy cream

Directions:

Heat the olive oil in a large pot over medium heat and sauté the onions, carrots, garlic and ginger until tender. Add in water and bring to a boil.

Reduce heat to low and simmer 30 minutes. Transfer the soup to a blender or food processor and blend, until smooth. Return to the pot and continue cooking for a few more minutes.

Remove soup from heat; stir in the cream. Serve with coriander sprinkled over each serving.

Sweet Potato Soup

Serves 6-7

Ingredients:

2 lb sweet potato, peeled, chopped

1 lb potatoes, peeled chopped

1 medium onions, chopped

4 cups chicken broth

5 tbsp olive oil

2 cloves garlic, minced

1 red chili pepper, finely chopped

salt and pepper, to taste

½ cup heavy cream

Directions:

Heat the olive oil in a large pot over medium heat and sauté the onions, garlic and chili pepper until just fragrant. Add the potatoes and sweet potatoes and add in the chicken broth. Bring to a boil.

Reduce heat to low and simmer 30 minutes or until potatoes are tender. Transfer the soup to a blender or food processor and blend, until smooth. Return to the pot and continue cooking for a few more minutes. Remove soup from heat; stir in the cream.

Irish Carrot Soup

Serves 5-6

Ingredients:

5-6 carrots, peeled, chopped

2 potatoes, peeled, chopped

1 small onion, chopped

4 cups chicken broth

3 tbsp olive oil

salt and pepper, to taste

1 cup sour cream, to serve

Directions:

Heat olive oil in a deep saucepan over medium-high heat and sauté the onion and carrot until tender. Add in potatoes and chicken broth.

Bring to the boil then reduce heat and simmer, partially covered, for 30 minutes, or until carrots are tender.

Set aside to cool then blend in batches until smooth. Return soup to saucepan and cook, stirring, for 4-5 minutes, or until heated through. Season with salt and pepper and serve with a dollop of cream.

Lentil, Buckwheat and Mushroom Soup

Serves 4-5

Ingredients:

2 medium leeks, trimmed, halved, sliced

10 white mushrooms, sliced

1/2 cup buckwheat groats (use either raw or toasted), rinsed

3 garlic cloves, cut

2 bay leaves

2 cans tomatoes chopped, undrained

3/4 cup red lentils

1/2 cup buckwheat groats (use either raw or toasted), rinsed

3 tbsp olive oil

1 tsp paprika

1 tsp savory

½ tsp cumin

salt and pepper, to taste

Directions:

Heat the oil in a large saucepan over medium-high heat. Gently sauté the leeks and mushrooms for 3-4 minutes or until softened. Add in cumin, paprika, savory and tomatoes, lentils, buckwheat, and 5 cups of cold water. Season with salt and pepper.

Cover and bring to the boil. Reduce heat to low. Simmer for 35-40 minutes, or until the buckwheat is tender.

Cream of Wild Mushroom Soup

Serves 4

Ingredients:

2 cups wild mushrooms, peeled and chopped

1 onion, chopped

2 cloves of garlic, crushed and chopped

1 tsp dried thyme

3 cups vegetable broth

salt and pepper, to taste

3 tbsp olive oil

Directions:

Sauté onions and garlic in a large soup pot till transparent. Add thyme and mushrooms.

Cook for 10 minutes then add the vegetable broth and simmer for another 10-20 minutes. Blend, season and serve.

Mediterranean Chickpea and Tomato Soup

Serves 10

Ingredients:

2 cups canned chickpeas, drained

a bunch of spring onions, finely cut

2 cloves garlic, crushed

1 cup canned tomatoes, diced

4 cups vegetable broth

3 tbsp olive oil

1 bay leaf

½ tsp rosemary

½ cup freshly grated Parmesan cheese

Directions:

Sauté onion and garlic in olive oil in a heavy soup pot. Add in broth, chickpeas, tomatoes, the bay leaf and rosemary.

Bring to the boil, then reduce heath and simmer for 20 minutes. Remove from heat and serve sprinkled with Parmesan cheese.

French-style Vegetable Soup

Serves 4-5

Ingredients:

1 leek, thinly sliced

1 large zucchini, diced

1 cup green beans, cut

2 garlic cloves, cut

4 cups vegetable broth

1 cup canned tomatoes, chopped

3.5 oz vermicelli, broken into small pieces

3 tbsp olive oil

black pepper, to the taste

4 tbsp freshly grated Parmesan cheese

Directions:

Heat the olive oil and gently sauté the leek, zucchini, green beans and garlic for about 5 minutes. Add in the vegetable broth. Stir in the tomatoes and bring to the boil, then reduce heat.

Add black pepper to taste and simmer for 10 minutes, or until the vegetables are tender but still holding their shape. Stir in the vermicelli.

Cover again and simmer for a further 5 minutes. Serve warm sprinkled with Parmesan cheese.

Minted Pea and Potato Soup

Serves 4

Ingredients:

1 onion, finely chopped

2 garlic cloves, finely chopped

4 cups vegetable broth

3-4 large potatoes, peeled and diced

1 lb green peas, frozen

1/3 cup mint leaves

3 tbsp olive oil

small mint leaves, to serve

Directions:

Heat oil in a large saucepan over medium-high heat and sauté onion and garlic for 5 minutes or until soft.

Add vegetable broth and bring to the boil, then add potatoes and mint. Cover, reduce heat, and cook for 15 minutes until tender. Add the peas 2 min before the end of the cooking time.

Remove from heat. Set aside to cool slightly, then blend soup, in batches, until smooth.

Return soup to saucepan over medium-low heat and cook until heated through. Season with salt and pepper.

Serve topped with mint leaves.

Brussels Sprout and Lentil Soup

Serves 4

Ingredients:

1 cup brown lentils

1 onion, chopped

2-3 cloves garlic, peeled

2 medium carrots, chopped

16 oz Brussels sprouts, shredded

4 cups chicken broth

4 tbsp olive oil

1 ½ tsp paprika

1 tsp summer savory

Directions:

Heat oil in a deep soup pot, add the onion and carrots and sauté until golden. Add in paprika and lentils with chicken broth.

Bring to the boil, lower heat and simmer for 15-20 minutes. Add the Brussels sprouts and the tomato to the soup, together with the garlic and summer savory. Cook for 15 more minutes, add salt to taste and serve.

Moroccan Lentil Soup

Serves 8-9

Ingredients:

1 cup red lentils

1/2 cup canned chickpeas, drained

2 onions, chopped

2 cloves garlic, minced

1 cup canned tomatoes, chopped

1/2 cup canned white beans, drained

3 carrots, diced

3 celery ribs, diced

6 cups water

1 tsp ginger, grated

1 tsp ground cardamom

½ tsp ground cumin

3 tbsp olive oil

Directions:

In a large soup pot, sauté onions, garlic and ginger in olive oil, for about 5 minutes. Add in the water, lentils, chickpeas, white beans, tomatoes, carrots, celery, cardamom and cumin.

Bring to a boil for a few minutes, then simmer for ½ hour or longer, until the lentils are tender. Puree half the soup in a food processor or blender. Return the pureed soup to the pot, stir and serve.

Curried Lentil Soup

Serves 5-6

Ingredients:

1 cup dried lentils

1 large onion, finely cut

1 celery rib, chopped

1 large carrot, chopped

3 garlic cloves, chopped

1 can tomatoes, undrained

3 cups vegetable broth

1 tbsp curry powder

1/2 tsp ground ginger

Directions:

Combine all ingredients in slow cooker.

Cover and cook on low for 5-6 hours.

Blend soup to desired consistency, adding additional hot water to thin, if desired.

Green Lentil Soup with Rice

Serves 6

Ingredients:

1 cup green lentils

1 small onion, finely cut

1 carrot, chopped

5 cups vegetable broth

1/4 cup rice

1 tbsp paprika

salt and black pepper, to taste

1/2 cup finely cut dill, to serve

Directions:

Heat oil in a large saucepan and sauté the onion stirring occasionally, until transparent. Add in carrot, paprika and lentils and stir to combine.

Add vegetable broth to the saucepan and bring to the boil, then reduce heat and simmer for 20 minutes.

Stir in rice and cook on medium low until rice is cooked. Sprinkle with dill and serve.

Simple Black Bean Soup

Serves 5-6

Ingredients:

1 cup dried black beans

5 cups vegetable broth

1 large onion, chopped

1 red pepper, chopped

1 tsp sweet paprika

1 tbsp dried mint

2 bay leaves

1 Serrano chili, finely chopped

1 tsp salt

4 tbsp fresh lime juice

1/2 cup chopped fresh cilantro

1 cup sour cream or yogurt, to serve

Directions:

Wash the beans and soak them in enough water overnight.

In a slow cooker, combine the beans and all other ingredients except for the lime juice and cilantro. Cover and cook on low for 7-8 hours.

Add salt, lime juice and fresh cilantro.

Serve with a dollop of sour cream or yogurt.

Bean and Pasta Soup

Serves 6-7

Ingredients:

1 cup small pasta, cooked

1 cup canned white beans, rinsed and drained

2 medium carrots, cut

1 cup fresh spinach, torn

1 medium onion, chopped

1 celery rib, chopped

2 garlic cloves, crushed

3 cups water

1 cup canned tomatoes, diced and undrained

1 cup vegetable broth

½ tsp rosemary

½ tsp basil

salt and pepper, to taste

Directions:

Add all ingredients except pasta and spinach into slow cooker. Cover and cook on low for 6-7 hours or high for 4 hours.

Add spinach and pasta about 30 minutes before the soup is finished cooking.

Slow Cooked Split Pea Soup

Serves 5-6

Ingredients:

1 lb dried green split peas, rinsed and drained

2 potatoes, peeled and diced

1 small onion, chopped

1 celery rib, chopped

1 carrot, chopped

2 garlic cloves, chopped

1 bay leaf

1 tsp black pepper

1/2 tsp salt

6 cups water

1 cup crumbled feta, to serve

Directions:

Combine all ingredients in slow cooker.

Cover and cook on low for 5-6 hours.

Discard bay leaf. Blend soup to desired consistency, adding additional hot water to thin, if desired.

Sprinkle feta cheese on top and serve with garlic or herb bread.

Spiced Citrus Bean Soup

Serves 6-7

Ingredients:

1 can (14 oz) white beans, rinsed and drained

2 medium carrots, cut

1 medium onion, chopped

1 tbsp gram masala

4 cups vegetable broth

1 cup coconut milk

1/2 tbsp grated ginger

juice of 1 orange

salt and pepper, to taste

1/2 cup fresh parsley leaves, finely cut, to serve

Directions:

In a large soup pot, sauté onions, carrots and ginger in olive oil, for about 5 minutes, stirring. Add gram masala and cook until just fragrant.

Add the orange juice and vegetable broth and bring to the boil. Simmer for about 10 min until the carrots are tender, then stir in the coconut milk.

Blend soup to desired consistency then add the beans and bring to a simmer. Serve sprinkled with parsley.

Slow Cooker Tuscan-style Soup

Serves 5-6

Ingredients:

1 lb potatoes, peeled and cubed

1 small onion, chopped

1 can mixed beans, drained

1 carrot, chopped

2 garlic cloves, chopped

4 cups vegetable broth

1 cups chopped kale

3 tbsp olive oil

1 bay leaf

salt and pepper, to taste

Parmesan cheese, to serve

Directions:

Heat oil in a skillet over medium heat and sauté the onion, carrot and garlic, stirring, for 2-3 minutes or until soft.

Combine all ingredients except the kale into the slow cooker. Season with salt and pepper to taste.

Cook on high for 4 hours or low for 6-7 hours. Add in kale about 30 minutes before soup is finished cooking. Serve sprinkled with Parmesan cheese.

Crock Pot Tomato Basil Soup

Serves: 5-6

Ingredients:

4 cups chopped fresh tomatoes or 27 oz can tomatoes

1/3 cup rice

3 cups water

1 large onion, diced

4 garlic cloves, minced

3 tbsp olive oil

1 tsp salt

1 tbsp dried basil

1 tbsp paprika

1 tsp sugar

½ bunch fresh parsley, to serve

Directions:

In a skillet, sauté onion and garlic for 2-3 minutes. When onions have softened, add them together with all other ingredients to the crock pot.

Cook on low for 5-7 hours, or on high for 3 1/2. Blend with an immersion blender and serve topped with fresh parsley.

Chunky Minestrone

Serves 4-5

Ingredients:

¼ cabbage, chopped

2 carrots, chopped

1 celery rib, thinly sliced

1 small onion, chopped

2 garlic cloves, chopped

2 tbsp olive oil

4 cups water

1 cup canned tomatoes, diced, undrained

1 cup fresh spinach, torn

½ cup pasta, cooked

black pepper and salt, to taste

Directions:

Heat olive oil and gently sauté carrots, cabbage, celery, onion and garlic for 5 minutes in a deep saucepan. Add in water, tomatoes and bring to a boil.

Reduce heat and simmer uncovered, for 20 minutes, or until vegetables are tender. Stir in spinach, macaroni, and season with pepper and salt to taste.

Cream of Tomato Soup

Serves: 5-6

Ingredients:

5 cups chopped fresh tomatoes

1/3 cup rice

3 cups water

1 large onion, diced

4 garlic cloves, minced

3 tbsp olive oil

1 tsp salt

1 tbsp paprika

1 tsp sugar

½ bunch fresh parsley, to serve

Directions:

Sauté onions and garlic in oil, in a large soup pot. When onions have softened, add tomatoes, stir in paprika and mix well to coat vegetables. Add in water.

Bring to a boil, lower heat and simmer for 15 minutes. Blend the soup, then return to the pot, add rice and a teaspoon of sugar. Bring to the boil again. Simmer for 15 minutes stirring occasionally. Sprinkle with parsley and serve.

Cauliflower Soup

Serves 4-5

Ingredients:

1 large onion, finely cut

1 medium head cauliflower, chopped

2-3 garlic cloves, minced

4 cups water

½ cup whole cream

4 tbsp olive oil

salt, to taste

fresh ground black pepper, to taste

Directions:

Heat the olive oil in a large pot over medium heat and sauté the onion, cauliflower and garlic. Stir in the water and bring the soup to a boil.

Reduce heat, cover, and simmer for 40 minutes. Remove the soup from heat, add the cream and blend in a blender. Season with salt and pepper.

Creamy Artichoke Soup

Serves 4

Ingredients:

1 can artichoke hearts, drained

3 cups vegetable broth

2 tbsp lemon juice

1 small onion, finely cut

2 cloves garlic, crushed

3 tbsp olive oil

2 tbsp flour

½ cup heavy cream

Directions:

Gently sauté the onion and garlic in some olive oil. Add the flour, whisking constantly, and then add the hot vegetable broth slowly, while still whisking. Cook for about 5 minutes.

Blend the artichoke, lemon juice, salt and pepper until smooth. Add the puree to the broth mix, stir well, and then stir in the cream. Cook until heated through. Garnish with a swirl of cream or a sliver of artichoke.

Tomato Artichoke Soup

Serves 4

Ingredients:

1 can artichoke hearts, drained

1 can diced tomatoes, undrained

3 cups vegetable broth

1 small onion, chopped

2 cloves garlic, crushed

1 tbsp pesto

black pepper, to taste

Directions:

Combine all ingredients in the slow cooker.

Cover and cook on low for 8-10 hours or on high for 4-5 hours.

Blend the soup in batches and return it to the slow cooker. Season with salt and pepper to taste and serve.

Creamy Artichoke and Horseradish Soup

Serves 4

Ingredients:

1 can artichoke hearts, drained

3 cups vegetable broth

1 tbsp horseradish sauce

2 tbsp lemon juice

1 small onion, finely cut

2 cloves garlic, crushed

3 tbsp olive oil

2 tbsp flour

½ cup heavy cream

2 tbsp chopped fresh chives plus extra to garnish

Directions:

Gently sauté the onion and garlic in some olive oil. Add in the flour, whisking constantly, and then add the hot vegetable broth slowly, while still whisking. Cook for about 5 minutes.

Blend the artichokes, salt and pepper until smooth. Add the puree to the broth mix, stir well, and then stir in the horseradish sauce and chopped chives.

Ladle the soup into bowls and top each with a tablespoon of the cream.

Roasted Red Pepper Soup

Serves 5-6

Ingredients:

5-6 large red peppers

1 large onion, chopped

2 garlic cloves, crushed

4 medium tomatoes, chopped

4 cups vegetable broth

3 tbsp olive oil

2 bay leaves

Directions:

Grill the peppers or roast them in the oven at 400 F until the skins are a little burnt. Place the roasted peppers in a brown paper bag or a lidded container and leave covered for about 10 minutes. This makes it easier to peel them. Peel the skins and remove the seeds. Cut the peppers in small pieces.

Heat oil in a large saucepan over medium-high heat. Add onion and garlic and sauté, stirring, for 3 minutes or until onion has softened. Add the red peppers, bay leaves, tomato and simmer for 5 minutes.

Add broth. Season with pepper. Bring to the boil, then reduce heat and simmer for 20 more minutes. Set aside to cool slightly. Blend, in batches, until smooth and serve.

Vietnamese Noodle Soup

Serves 4

Ingredients:

9 oz rice stick noodles

4 cups vegetable broth

1 lemongrass stem, only pale part, finely chopped

2 garlic cloves, cut

½ tsp ground ginger

1 long red chili, thinly sliced

3.5 oz shiitake mushrooms

1 cup bean sprouts

4 tbsp lime juice

coriander and mint leaves, to garnish

Directions:

Pour boiling water over the noodles and leave aside for 10 minutes, or until soft. Place the vegetable broth, lemongrass, garlic, ginger, chili and 3 cups of water in a large saucepan.

Bring to the boil, then reduce heat to medium. Simmer for 10 minutes. Add in mushrooms and cook for 5 more minutes, then stir in the lime juice. Divide the noodles and bean sprouts among bowls. Serve the soup topped with coriander and mint leaves.

Old-Fashioned Spinach Soup

Serves 4-5

Ingredients:

1 lb spinach, frozen

1 large onion or 4-5 spring onions, finely cut

1 carrot, chopped

3 cups water

3-4 tbsp olive oil

1/4 cup white rice

1-2 cloves garlic, crushed

1 tbsp paprika

black pepper, to taste

salt, to taste

Directions:

Chop the onion and spinach. Heat the oil in a cooking pot and add the onion and carrot. Sauté for a few minutes, until just softened. Add in the chopped garlic, paprika, and rice and stir for a minute. Remove from heat.

Add the chopped spinach along with about 2 cups of hot water and season with salt and pepper. Bring back to a boil, then reduce the heat and simmer for around 15 minutes.

Spinach, Nettle and Feta Cheese Soup

Serves 6

Ingredients:

1 lb frozen spinach, thawed

13 oz nettles, young top shoots

3.5 oz feta cheese

1 large onion or 4-5 scallions

2 -3 tbsp light cream

3-4 tbsp olive oil

¼ cup white rice

1-2 cloves garlic

4 cups water

black pepper, to taste

salt, to taste

Directions:

Clean the young nettles, wash and cook them in slightly salted water. Drain, rinse, drain again, chop them and leave aside.

Heat the oil in a cooking pot, add the onion, garlic and paprika and sauté for a few minutes, stirring constantly. Remove from heat. Add the spinach and nettles. Add about 4 cups of hot water and season with salt and pepper. Bring back to the boil, then reduce the heat and simmer for around 30 minutes.

In the meantime crumble the cheese with a fork. When the soup is ready stir in the crumbled feta cheese and the cream. Serve hot.

Nettle Soup

Serves 6

Ingredients:

1.5 lb young top shoots of nettles, well washed

3-4 tbsp sunflower oil

2 potatoes, diced small

1 bunch spring onions, coarsely chopped

3 cups hot water

1 tsp salt

Directions:

Clean the young nettles, wash and cook them in slightly salted water. Drain, rinse, drain again and then chop or pass through a sieve.

Sauté the chopped spring onions and potatoes in the oil until the potatoes start to color a little.

Turn off the heat, add the nettles, then gradually stir in the water. Stir well, then simmer until the potatoes are cooked through.

Celery Root Soup

Serves 4

Ingredients:

2 leeks (white and light green parts only), chopped

2 garlic cloves, crushed

1 large celery root, peeled and diced

2 potatoes, peeled and diced

4 cups vegetable broth

1 bay leaf

2 tbsp olive oil

salt and black pepper, to taste

Directions:

In a skillet, heat olive oil, then add the leeks and sauté about 3-4 minutes. Add in the garlic and sauté an additional 3-40 seconds.

In a slow cooker, add the sautéed leeks and garlic, celeriac, potatoes, broth, bay leaf, salt, and pepper. Cover and cook on low heat for 7-8 hours. Set aside to cool, remove the bay leaf, then process in a blender or with an immersion blender until smooth.

Sweet Potato and Coconut Soup

Serves: 4-5

Ingredients:

1 onion, finely cut

1 garlic clove, crushed

2 large sweet potatoes, peeled and diced

3-4 cups vegetable broth

1 can coconut milk

3 tbsp olive oil

1/2 tsp nutmeg

Directions:

Heat olive oil in a large saucepan over medium heat. Add in onion and sauté until tender. Add in the garlic and cook until just fragrant. Stir in broth, sweet potato and nutmeg.

Bring the soup to a boil then reduce heat and simmer, covered, for 30 minutes. Blend until smooth and cook for 2-3 minutes until heated through.

Red Lentil and Quinoa Soup

Serves 4-5

Ingredients:

½ cup quinoa

1 cup red lentils

5 cups water

1 onion, chopped

2-3 garlic cloves, chopped

1 red bell pepper, finely cut

1 small tomato, chopped

3 tbsp olive oil

1 tsp ginger

1 tsp cumin

1 tbsp paprika

salt and black pepper, to taste

Directions:

Rinse quinoa and lentils very well in a fine mesh strainer under running water and set aside to drain.

In a large soup pot, heat the olive oil over medium heat. Add the onion, garlic and red pepper and sauté for 1-2 minutes until just fragrant. Stir in paprika, spices, red lentils and quinoa.

Add in water and gently bring to a boil then lower heat and simmer, covered, for 30 minutes. Add the chopped tomato and salt and cook for 5 minutes more. Blend the soup and serve.

Spinach, Leek and Quinoa Soup

Serves 6

Ingredients:

½ cup quinoa

2 leeks, halved lengthwise and sliced

1 onion, chopped

2 garlic cloves, chopped

1 can tomatoes, diced, undrained

2 cups of fresh spinach leaves, cut

2 cups vegetable broth

3 cups water

2 tbsp sunflower oil

1 tsp paprika

salt and pepper, to taste

3-4 tbsp lemon juice, to serve

Directions:

Heat a large soup pot over medium heat. Add oil and onion and sauté for 2 minutes. Add in leeks and cook for another 2-3 minutes, then add garlic and paprika and stir. Season with salt and black pepper to taste.

Add the vegetable broth, water, canned tomatoes, and quinoa.

Bring the soup to a boil then reduce heat and simmer for 15 minutes. Stir in the spinach and cook for another 5 minutes. Serve with lemon juice

Leek, Quinoa and Potato Soup

Serves 6

Ingredients:

½ cup quinoa

4 cups water

2-3 potatoes, diced

1 small onion, cut

1 leek, halved lengthwise and sliced

3 tbsp olive oil

lemon juice, to taste

Directions:

Heat a soup pot over medium heat. Add olive oil and onion and sauté for 2 minutes. Add in leeks and potatoes, stir, and cook for a few minutes more.

Add water, bring to a boil, reduce heat and simmer for 5 minutes. Add in the very well washed quinoa and simmer for 10 minutes. Serve with lemon juice to taste.

Garden Quinoa Soup

Serves 6

Ingredients:

½ cup quinoa

1 onion, chopped

1 potato, diced

1 carrot, diced

1 red bell pepper, chopped

2 tomatoes, chopped

1 zucchini, diced

4-5 cups water

1 tsp paprika

1 tsp summer savory

3-4 tbsp olive oil

2 tbsp fresh lemon juice

Directions:

Rinse quinoa very well in a fine mesh strainer under running water and set aside to drain.

Heat the oil in a large soup pot and gently sauté the onions and carrot for 2-3 minutes, stirring every now and then. Add paprika, savory, potato, bell pepper, tomatoes and water. Stir to combine.

Cover, bring to a boil, then lower heat and simmer for 10 minutes. Add in the quinoa and zucchini; stir, cover and simmer for 15 minutes, or until the vegetables are tender. Add in the lemon juice; stir to combine and serve.

Quinoa, White Bean, and Kale Soup

Serves 5-6

Ingredients:

½ cup uncooked quinoa, rinsed well

1 small onion, chopped

1 can diced tomatoes, undrained

2 cans cannellini beans, undrained

3 cups chopped kale

2 garlic cloves, chopped

4 cups vegetable broth

1 tsp paprika

1 tsp dried mint

salt and pepper, to taste

Directions:

Combine all ingredients except the kale into the slow cooker. Season with salt and pepper to taste.

Cook on high for 4 hours or low for 6-7 hours. Add in kale about 30 minutes before soup is finished cooking.

FREE BONUS RECIPES: 10 Natural Homemade Beauty Recipes that are Easy on the Budget

Dry Skin Body Scrub

Ingredients:

½ cup brown sugar

½ cup sea salt salt

2-3 tbsp honey

2 tbsp argan oil

2 tbsp fresh orange juice

Directions:

Mix all ingredients until you have a smooth paste. Apply to wet skin and exfoliate body in small, circular motions.

Rinse with warm water.

Lavender Body Scrub Recipe

Ingredients:

1/2 cup sugar

2 tbsp lavender leaves

¼ cup jojoba oil

3 drops lavender essential oil

Directions:

Combine sugar and lavender leaves. Add jojoba oil and lavender essential oil. Apply the mixture to damp skin.

Gently exfoliate in small, circular motions. Rinse with warm water.

Rosemary Body Scrub

Ingredients:

1/2 cup coconut oil

1/2 cup sugar

1/4 cup flax seeds

7-8 drops Rosemary Essential Oil

Directions:

Combine sugar and flax seeds and stir until mixed well. Add the coconut oil and mix until evenly combined.

Apply the mixture to damp skin. Gently exfoliate in small, circular motions. Rinse with warm water.

Banana-Sugar Body Scrub

Ingredients:

1 ripe banana

4 tbsp raw sugar

1 tbsp cocoa powder

2 tbsp almond oil

¼ tsp pure vanilla extract

Directions:

Smash ingredients together with a fork.

Gently massage over your body for a few minutes. Rinse off with warm water

Coffee Body Scrub

Ingredients:

1/4 cup ground coffee

1/4 cup sugar

3 tbsp olive oil

1 vitamin E capsule

Directions:

Mix sugar with ground coffee, olive oil and the Vitamin E capsule.

Apply over wet body and massage gently. Rinse off with warm water.

Strained Yogurt Face Mask

Ingredients:

5 tbsp plain yogurt

1 slice of white bread

Directions:

This is a very old family recipe and is also the easiest basic face mask. It was used probably by every Bulgarian mother and grandmother back in the days when there were no commercial creams and moisturizers.

Place the slice of bread in a plate, put the yogurt on top of it, spread it evenly and leave in the fridge for a few hours or overnight.

In the morning take the strained yogurt and spread it on your clean face, leave it for 20 minutes and rinse it with water. Results are always excellent.

Oats Bran Face Mask

Ingredients:

3 tbsp oats bran

hot water

2 drops Bulgarian rose essential oil

Directions:

Boil bran in 1/2 cup of water. Strain, cool, add rose oil and apply to face.

Leave for 15 minutes and wash with lukewarm water.

Pear and Honey Mask

Ingredients:

1 ripe pear

1 tbsp honey

1 tsp sour cream

Directions:

Peel and cut the pear, then mash it with a fork into a smooth paste. Stir in a tablespoon of honey and a teaspoon of cream.

Spread the mixture evenly over your face and neck. Leave it for 10 minutes then rinse off.

Banana Nourishing Mask

Ingredients:

1 banana

1 tsp honey

1 tsp plain yogurt

Directions:

Mash a banana, add the honey and the yogurt, mix well and spread it evenly on a clean face.

Leave it for at least 15 minutes and wash with cold water.

Apple Autumn Mask

Ingredients:

1/2 apple

1 tsp oatmeal

1 tsp honey

Directions:

Take a ripe half apple, grate it and mash it with a fork. Add one teaspoon oatmeal and one teaspoon honey to it and stir well.

Spread on face and leave it on until the mixture dries completely then rinse it off with ordinary water.

About the Author

Vesela lives in Bulgaria with her family of six (including the Jack Russell Terrier). Her passion is going green in everyday life and she loves to prepare homemade cosmetic and beauty products for all her family and friends.

Vesela has been publishing her cookbooks for over a year now. If you want to see other healthy family recipes that she has published, together with some natural beauty books, you can check out her [Author Page](#) on Amazon.

Made in the USA
Middletown, DE
26 January 2023

23128494R00059